Plan Prepare COOK

Tasty
Drinks and Snacks

Rita Storey

W
FRANKLIN WATTS
LONDON • SYDNEY

Contents

First published in 2011 by
Franklin Watts
338 Euston Road
London NW1 3BH

Franklin Watts Australia
Level 17/207 Kent Street
Sydney NSW 2000

© Franklin Watts 2011
Series editor: Sarah Peutrill
Art director: Jonathan Hair

Series designed and created for Franklin Watts
by Storeybooks
Designer: Rita Storey
Editor: Nicola Barber
Photography: Tudor Photography

A CIP catalogue record for this book is available
from the British Library
Printed in China

Dewey classification: 641.5'2

ISBN 978 1 4451 0111 8

Picture credits
All photographs Tudor Photography, Banbury
unless otherwise stated. Shutterstock p5;
Wishlistimages.co.uk p4

Cover images Tudor Photography
All photos posed by models. Thanks to Jack Abbott,
Amy Mobley, Serish Begum and Jordan McElavaine.

Franklin Watts is a division of Hachette Children's
Books, an Hachette UK company
www.hachette.co.uk

Pages marked with have a related free downloadable activity sheet at www.franklinwatts/downloads. Find out more on page 32.

Words in **bold** are in the glossary on page 30.

Before you start

- Wash your hands before and after preparing food.
- Ask an adult to help when the recipe uses the cooker or grill.
- If you have long hair, clip or tie it back.
- Dry your hands before you plug in or unplug any electrical appliances.
- Wear an apron or an old shirt.
- Wash up as you go along.
- Be extra careful with sharp knives.
- Ask an adult to help with the liquidiser/food processor.
- Ask an adult to help you weigh the ingredients.

Look out for this useful guide to each recipe.

How long each recipe takes to make.

How difficult each recipe is to make.

If the food needs to be cooked.

All about snacks and drinks

Snacks and drinks are a useful way of boosting your energy between meals. But eating too many snacks can stop you being hungry and eating properly at meal times.

Processed foods

Supermarkets sell a wide range of foods made in handy sizes to eat as snacks. Many of these **processed foods** are high in sugar and **fat**. Some also have **artificial colourings** and **flavourings** to make them look and taste more attractive. It's best to eat them only very occasionally.

Your diet

What you eat and drink is called your **diet**. There are lots of different foods and drinks to choose from. Try not to eat crisps and processed snacks every day. There are lots of healthy snacks that are equally delicious.

The human machine

The human body is like a machine that needs **energy** to work. Energy is released from the food you eat and used up by your body. Energy is measured in **joules** or **calories**.

A healthy balance

To be healthy you must eat enough food to produce the energy needed by your body. But if you eat more food than your body actually requires, it is turned into fat.

If you do this all the time, you keep getting fatter.

When you **exercise** you use up energy. Playing a sport, walking, riding your bike or dancing are all good ways to burn off energy and have fun at the same time.

Milk, cheese and yoghurt

These foods contain **protein**. They are convenient foods to eat or drink as a snack.
• Look at the labels on yoghurts and choose the ones that are lowest in sugar and fat.
• Choose low-fat cheese.

Nuts and beans

These foods contain protein.
• Nuts are a good snack but they are high in fat, so try not to eat too many. Nuts without salt are healthier than salted nuts.

Walking to school instead of taking the bus is a good way to get some daily exercise. It gives you more time to chat to your friends too!

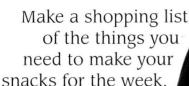

Make a shopping list of the things you need to make your snacks for the week.

Check the labels

Many **savoury** snacks are high in salt and fat. Many sweet snacks and drinks are high in sugar.

Look at the labels on packets for low-salt, low-sugar and low-fat foods (particularly if the fat is **saturated fat**).

A healthy alternative

Snacks and drinks can add a lot of extra calories to the amount you eat every day. To stop yourself reaching for salty or

sugary snacks and drinks too often, make sure you have a healthy alternative available. Fruit, breadsticks, raw vegetables, nuts and water are a good choice.

Make your own snacks

You can also make your own snacks. That way you know exactly what you are eating. Tasty dips and mini-wraps can be kept in the fridge for a few days.

'Snacking' can become a habit. Before you reach for a snack, stop and think. Are you really hungry – or just bored?!

Starchy foods

You should eat **starchy** foods every day – they should make up about a third of what you eat. To eat a starchy food as a snack, try breadsticks and a dip (see pages 12–13). A bowl of cereal also makes a good snack.

Water is the most natural drink there is.

Water

You need water for your body to perform well. You get some water from the foods you eat. You should drink six to eight glasses of water a day – more in hot weather. A glass of water can help you feel full and stop you craving snacks.

Pizza muffin

This filling snack is quick and easy to make. You can try the topping suggested here, or use your favourite pizza topping.

You will need

- kitchen knife
- plate

Ingredients

- 1 English muffin, split in half and toasted
- 2 tablespoons tomato pizza sauce

Topping
- a few strips of red, green or yellow pepper
- a few thin slices of mushroom (see page 28)
- 30 g (1 oz) mozzarella or low-fat Cheddar cheese, grated (see page 29)

This makes a snack for 1 or 2 people.

1

- Spread a tablespoon of the tomato sauce on to the cut side of each toasted muffin.

2

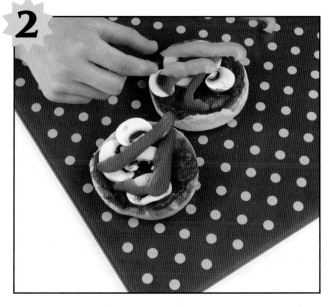

- Divide the topping between the two halves.

- Sprinkle half of the cheese on top of each muffin.
- **Grill** for 2 minutes or until the cheese has melted and is golden brown.

If you prefer

Try any of these toppings for a change:

- strips of cooked ham
- chopped, cooked chicken
- slices of courgette
- pieces of cooked bacon
- pineapple
- pepperoni

Delicious!

10 minutes

Easy

Cooked

9

Mini-wraps

These tasty little treats can be stuffed with all sorts of fillings. Experiment with a few different ones! Make up a batch and keep them in the fridge ready for a 'snack attack'.

Ingredients

- 1 wrap
- 1 tablespoon cream cheese

Filling of your choice:
- thin slices of ham, chicken salami, cucumber or tomato

You will need

- chopping board
- kitchen knife

If you prefer

You can use a thin layer of peanut butter instead of cream cheese.

1

- Place the wrap on the chopping board.
- Spread the cream cheese all over the wrap.

2

- Place the slices of meat along the middle of the wrap.

3

4

5

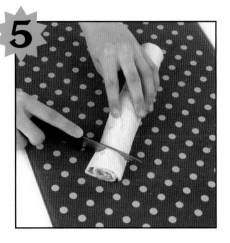

- Place the rest of the filling all around the wrap.

- Roll into a tight roll.

- Cut into 2.5-cm (1-in) lengths.

Scrummy!

Handy hint
These rolls work best if the filling inside is not too chunky.

10 minutes

Very easy

No cooking

11

Cheese dip

This tasty dip makes an ideal snack when you get home from school. Have everything ready in the fridge so that you can eat it straight away.

You will need

- small mixing bowl
- tablespoon
- small serving bowl
- plate

Types of cheeses
These cheeses have a creamy texture: cream cheese, fromage frais, ricotta, mozzarella
Soft cheese has a soft, sticky texture: Brie, Camembert
Hard cheese can be grated: Cheddar, Parmesan

Ingredients

- 4 tablespoons cream cheese
- 2 tablespoons mayonnaise
- 1 tablespoon chopped fresh chives
- sticks of carrot, celery and cucumber
- breadsticks
- pitta bread cut into strips
- tortilla chips

1

- Measure the cream cheese and mayonnaise into a bowl.

2

- Stir until mixed.

- Add the chopped herbs.

- Spoon the mixture into a serving bowl.

- Arrange the vegetable sticks, breadsticks, pitta bread strips and tortilla chips round the bowl.

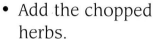

Handy hint

Remember – if you are sharing the dip with someone else always break off small pieces and dip those. Never put something into the dip after you have taken a bite out of it.

Get dipping!

10 minutes

Easy

No cooking

13

Fruits and nuts

Dried fruits and nuts are a filling snack. There are lots of different ones to choose from. Try as many as you can and see which you like, then combine them to make your own special mix.

Dried fruits

Cranberries

Raisins

Banana

Coconut

Apricots

Papaya

Nuts

Brazil nuts

Hazelnuts

Pecan nuts

Almonds

Walnuts

Handy hint
Keep some little bags or pots handy to fill with a handful of your special mix.

Go nuts!

5 minutes

Easy

No cooking

15

Blueberry milkshake
or smoothie

A milkshake is made with milk, fruit and ice cream. A smoothie is made from juice, milk, yoghurt and fruit. Both are equally delicious – take your pick!

Ingredients

Milkshake
- 2 scoops vanilla ice cream
- 300 ml (10 fl oz) milk
- 150g (5½ oz) blueberries

Smoothie
- 175 ml (6 fl oz) apple juice
- 125 ml (4 fl oz) plain yoghurt
- 1 banana, peeled and sliced
- 150g (5½ oz) blueberries

You will need

Milkshake
- ice cream scoop
- liquidiser
- glass and drinking straw

Smoothie
- liquidiser
- glass and drinking straw

Milkshake

1 • Put the ice cream and milk into the liquidiser.

2 • Add the blueberries.

3 • Whizz until smooth.

Smoothie

- Measure the apple juice into the liquidiser.

- Add the yoghurt, banana and blueberries.

- Whizz until smooth.

Milkshake and smoothie

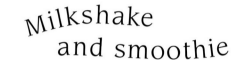

- Pour into a glass, add a straw and enjoy a great-tasting drink.

Mmm!

If you prefer

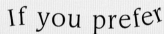

Strawberries, raspberries, ripe mango or peach also work well in a milkshake or smoothie.

5 minutes

Easy

No cooking

Tropical fizz
and fruity ice cubes

This drink is full of **tropical fruit** flavours. Tropical fruits include papayas, mangoes, bananas and pineapples. If you prefer, you can use orange juice instead of tropical fruit juice.

You will need
- jug
- ice-cube tray
- sieve
- bowl
- freezer
- glass and drinking straw

Ingredients

For the ice cubes:
- 568 ml (1 pint) water, boiled and left to cool (you can use plain cold water, but boiled water makes the ice cubes very clear)
- small tin tropical fruit salad in fruit juice

For the 'fizz':
- 1 litre (1¾ pints) tropical fruit juice (fresh if possible)
- 1 bottle sparkling water
- a few mint leaves (optional)
- paper umbrellas to decorate (optional)

1
- Half fill the ice-cube tray with the cooled boiled water.

2
- Rest the sieve on the bowl and tip in the fruit. Leave to drain.

3
- Put a piece of fruit into each ice-cube compartment. Freeze overnight until hard.

18

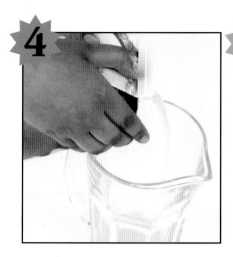

4

- When your ice cubes are ready, prepare the 'fizz'.
- In the jug, mix the fruit juice and sparkling water.

5

- Mix in the rest of the tropical fruit and the fruit juice.

6

- Remove the ice cubes from the tray.
- Put them in the jug and leave it to get really cold.

Serve the drink with a straw and paper umbrella for decoration.

Fizzylicious!

'Fizz':
 5 minutes
Ice cubes:
 overnight

Easy

No cooking

Lemonade
in a frosted glass

To make this refreshing lemonade extra special, serve it in a pretty, sugar-frosted glass.

Ingredients

Per person
- 1 lemon
- 568 ml (1 pint) water
- 1 tablespoon sugar or honey
- lemon juice and sugar for frosting the glass
- ice cubes (optional)

Citrus fruits
Lemons, oranges, mandarins grapefruit, limes and tangerines are all **citrus fruits**. These fruits contain lots of juice and **vitamin C**. This vitamin is important to keep your body healthy.

- Cut the lemon into slices on the chopping board

- Put the lemon slices into the jug.

- Add the sugar.

Ask an adult to:
- boil some water in a kettle and measure 568 ml (1 pint) into a jug.
- pour the water over the lemons and sugar.

- Stir, then leave in the fridge for a couple of hours until the lemonade is very cold.

- Dip the rim of the glass in lemon juice, then into some sugar.

Beautiful!

- Top up the glasses with ice-cold lemonade and enjoy a delicious refreshing drink.

| 2 hours |
| Easy |
| No cooking |

Fruity yoghurt cone

Try this fruity yoghurt to cool you down on a hot day. The added fruit means it is also part of your 5-a-day (see page 6).

Ingredients
- ice-cream cone
- 2 tablespoons fresh fruit, cut into pieces
- 1 scoop shop-bought frozen yoghurt
- maple syrup or runny honey
- chopped nuts

Types of yoghurt
Yoghurt is made from cows' milk, sheep's milk or goats' milk. The milk is gently heated and thickened to make yoghurt.

Natural yoghurt does not have anything added to it.

Fruit yoghurt has fruit and often sugar added.

Low-fat yoghurt has had some of the fat removed from it.

You will need
- tablespoon
- ice-cream scoop

1

- Put the fruit in the bottom of the cone.

2

- Top with a scoop of frozen yoghurt.

- Decorate with a small whole fruit or a piece of a larger fruit.

- Drizzle a little syrup or honey on the top.

- Top with a sprinkle of chopped nuts.

Scrumptious

2 minutes

Easy

No cooking

23

Hot chocolate

As an occasional treat on a cold winter's day this hot chocolate is a wonderful creamy drink.

You will need

- small saucepan
- tablespoon
- wooden spoon
- 2 mugs
- tea strainer or small sieve

Ingredients

- 1 tablespoon cocoa powder or drinking chocolate
- 250 ml (9 fl oz) milk

To serve:
- a few mini marshmallows
- a small pot of double cream whipped until thick (see page 29)

This serves 2 people.

Milk

Most milk is **pasteurised**. This means that it is heated to destroy any harmful **bacteria**.

Whole milk has nothing added or removed.

Semi-skimmed milk has half of the fat taken out.

Skimmed milk has most of the fat taken out.

- In a saucepan mix the cocoa with one tablespoon of the milk to make a paste.

- Stir in the rest of the milk.
- Turn the hob to medium.

- Heat the milk and cocoa over a low heat until the mixture begins to bubble.
- Turn off the hob.

- Pour into 2 mugs.

- Top with a spoonful of whipped cream.
- Sprinkle on the marshmallows.

- Put a small amount of cocoa powder in the tea strainer and shake a little on top of the cream and marshmallows.

Mmmmm

Handy hint
Be careful not to drink the chocolate until it has cooled a little.

10 minutes

Easy

Cooked

Mini banana cakes

These easy-to-make, squidgy cakes are just the thing to give you a boost of energy.

Ingredients

80 g (3 oz) butter
2 small, ripe bananas
2 medium eggs
125 ml (4 fl oz) milk
250 g (9 oz) self-raising flour
1 teaspoon baking powder
½ teaspoon bicarbonate of soda
115 g (4 oz) caster sugar

Topping:
• toffee sauce and chopped nuts

You will need

• small saucepan
• wooden spoon
• 3 bowls
• fork
• whisk
• sieve
• mixing spoon
• 2 teaspoons
• cup-cake or muffin tray
• cake cases
• cooling rack

Before you start

• Turn the oven on to 190°C (375°F).

1

• Turn the hob on to low.
• Put the butter into the saucepan. Heat until it is melted.

2

• Mash the bananas with a fork.

3

• Whisk the eggs (see page 29). Add the eggs to the mashed banana.
• Pour on the milk.
• Mix together.

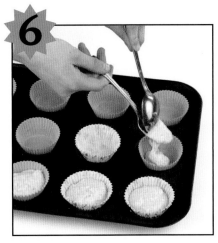

- Sieve the flour, baking powder and bicarbonate of soda into a bowl.
- Add the sugar.

- Add the egg, milk and banana mixture to the flour mixture.
- Mix them together with a mixing spoon.

- Put the cake cases into the tray.
- Spoon teaspoons of the mixture into the cases.
- **Bake** the cakes in the oven for 25 minutes.
- Cool them on a wire rack.

- Drizzle on a little toffee sauce and sprinkle with chopped nuts.

Yummmmm

| 50 minutes |
| Medium |
| Cooked |

How to!

Slice

Slicing is preparing something by cutting a thin piece from it. You can slice lots of different foods including bread, cheese, cucumber, tomatoes, fruits, vegetables and meat.

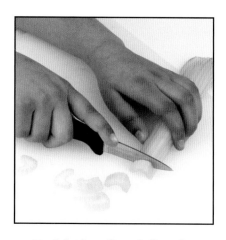

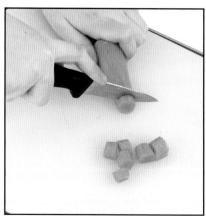

- Hold the food firmly. Do not hold too close to the end you are cutting.

- Cut across the food using a sawing action.

Chop

Chopping is cutting something into lots of equal-sized pieces. How small the pieces are depends on what you are cooking. Nuts, fruits and meat can all be chopped.

- Some things such as nuts need to be chopped very finely. You can do this in a food processor or liquidiser.

- To chop into larger chunks first take off a thick slice. Cut the slice into pieces first one way, and then the other.

Beat, whisk or whip

To beat means to stir a mixture quickly to combine everything together.

If the mixture is liquid you stir it by whisking or whipping.

Whisking and whipping add air to a mixture to make it lighter.

Double or whipping cream is whipped to make it thick.

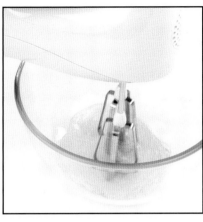

- Beating egg whites is much quicker using an electric mixer.

- If the mixture is liquid, for example eggs, use a fork or whisk.

Grate

A food grater has lots of sharp blades that can turn food into strips.

A box grater has different-sized blades for different foods.

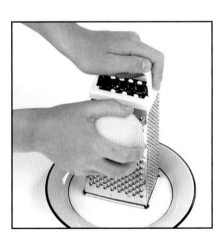

- Cheese and carrots are best grated on the largest blades.

- Hold the top of the grater, press the food against the blades and push down.

- The smallest blades are for grating the rind off oranges and lemons.

Glossary

artificial colouring A manufactured colouring added to food.

artificial flavouring Manufactured flavours that are added to food.

bacteria Tiny, single-celled micro-organisms.

bake To cook in an oven with heat all round the food.

calorie A measurement of the energy in food.

citrus fruit A type of fruit. The best-known citrus fruits are oranges, lemons, grapefruit and limes.

decay To go bad or rot.

diet The things that you eat and drink.

energy A type of power that can be used. Food is changed to energy in your body.

exercise Physical activity that uses up calories (energy) and improves fitness.

fat 1. A greasy substance found in food. Fats in food are divided into two types: **saturated fats** are found in cream, cheese, butter, suet, lard, fatty meat and chocolate; **unsaturated fats** are found in avocados, nuts, vegetable oils and olive oils. Unsaturated fats are healthier than saturated fats.
2. Tissue in the human body where energy is stored.

grill A way of cooking food using direct heat from above or below.

joule A measurement of energy.

pasteurised Milk that is pasteurised has been heated for a short time to kill any bacteria that could cause food poisoning. Pasteurising milk also helps it to last longer.

processed food Any food product that has been changed in some way. Cooking, freezing, drying, canning and preserving are all methods of processing food. Processed foods may contain colourings, flavourings and other additives and preservatives.

protein A substance found in some foods. It is needed by the body to grow and develop properly. Meat, eggs, milk, nuts and some types of bean contain protein.

savoury A taste that is salty or spicy.

semi-skimmed Describes a type of milk that has had half of the cream (fat) removed.

starchy Describes a food that contains starch. Starchy foods make up one of the food groups. They include bread, cereals, rice, pasta and potatoes.

tropical fruit A fruit grown in a part of the world called the tropics where there are no frosts. Tropical fruits include papayas, mangoes, bananas and pineapples.

vitamin C One of the substances that are essential in very small amounts in the body for normal growth and activity. Vitamin C is found in fresh fruits and vegetables.

Equipment

chopping board

little sieve/tea strainer

big sieve

cake cases

measuring jug

wire cooling rack

ice-cube tray

mixing spoon

whisk

mixing bowl

grater

non-stick saucepan

small sharp knife

kitchen knife

tablespoon

dessertspoon

teaspoon

ice-cream scoop

You will also need:
tea-towel
weighing scales
oven gloves
cup-cake tray

wooden spoons

liquidiser

food processor

Index

Activity sheets

The following pages have accompanying sheets which are available to download for free at www.franklinwatts.co.uk.

Pages 4–5 All about snacks and drinks
Plan your snacks and drinks for the week ahead on this handy food chart. Fill in the shopping list so you know what you need to buy.

Pages 6–7 All about snacks and drinks
What drinks and snack do your friends like best? Fill in this food survey to find out which are the most popular.

Page 31 Equipment
Download a colourful poster of all the equipment used in the 'Plan Prepare Cook' books.